SANTA MARIA PUBLIC LIBRARY

Indexed

Discarded by
Santa Maria Library

j970.01   POOLE, FREDERICK KING
             EARLY EXPLORATION
         OF NORTH AMERICA.
         c1989

89
↯↯↯
95
96
100

90
91

92

94

99

91

93
97

02

DEMCO

EARLY EXPLORATION
OF NORTH AMERICA

Also by
Frederick King Poole

An Album of Modern China
Mao Zedong

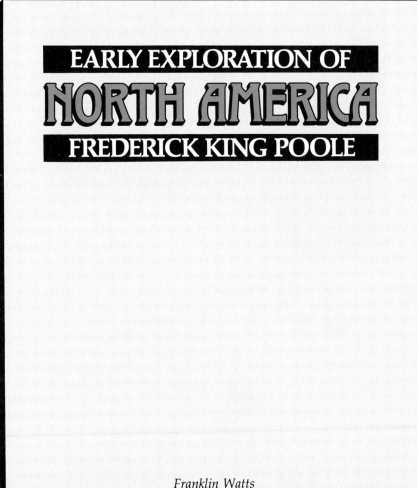

EARLY EXPLORATION OF
NORTH AMERICA
FREDERICK KING POOLE

Franklin Watts
New York/London/Toronto/Sydney
A First Book/1989

Cover photograph courtesy of The Granger Collection

Photographs courtesy of:
The Granger Collection: pp. 10, 13, 15, 20, 23,
26, 28, 29, 34, 41, 44, 49, 53, 54, 57, 58;
New York Public Library Picture collection: p. 46.

Library of Congress Cataloging in Publication Data

Poole, Frederick King.
Early exploration of North America / by Frederick King Poole.
p.   cm. — (A First book)
Bibliography: p.
Includes index.
Summary: Describes the exploration of North America by European
seafarers in the fifteenth and sixteenth centuries, including
discussion of the Vikings, Columbus, John Cabot, the early Spanish
and French explorers, and the search for the Northwestern Passage.
ISBN 0-531-10683-7
1. America — Discovery and exploration — Juvenile literature.
2. Explorers — North America — History — Juvenile literature.
[1. America — Discovery and exploration.] I. Title. II. Series.
E101.P66   1989
970.01 — dc19   88-30382   CIP   AC

Copyright © 1989 by Frederick King Poole
All rights reserved
Printed in the United States of America
6   5   4   3   2   1

CONTENTS

1 PRELUDE: THE FIRST DISCOVERY

Native Americans, whom Europeans later called "Indians," probably came originally from Central Asia. It is now believed they crossed the Bering Sea from Siberia to Alaska, either by raft or by using a bridge of land that no longer exists.

It is believed these migrations took place during the Ice Age, at least 20,000 years ago. People from Central Asia could thus be considered the earliest known people to have "discovered" the Americas.

But this was at a time when events were not recorded for history. When we talk about the discovery of North and South America, we usually mean discovery by people from advanced civilizations much closer to our own time. The first sighting for which we have clear written records was by Christopher Columbus nearly 500 years ago. However, folk tales and legends indicate the Americas were seen by other seafarers long before Columbus. The first sighting has been attributed to, among others, the Welsh and Irish from the British Isles, the Phoenicians from the Middle East, and sailors from China and Africa.

A discovery for which we have some evidence took place in what is now eastern Canada around the end of the tenth century and the beginning of the eleventh. It was by people called Vikings, who came from the area called Scandinavia in the far north of Europe. They had become the most adventurous, and most feared, seafarers of Europe. In their small open ships, they had been staging raids as far south as the Mediterranean Sea. In the north, they had conquered much of Ireland and sailed west into the Atlantic to the Faroes, Iceland, and then Greenland.

Other sailors in Europe hardly ever went out of sight of land. The Vikings, though they did not have the compass, had crude devices that helped them navigate by what they saw in the sky. When there was no familiar land in sight, they steered their ships by observing the position of the sun in the daytime and the North Star at night.

Viking settlements in Greenland, the last stop west before North America, were established by about A.D. 985 by a renegade known as Eric the Red. Because of his violent behavior, he had been banished first from his native Norway and later from the Viking settlements in Iceland.

About fifteen years later Eric's son, Leif Ericson, and a crew of thirty-five sailed west to barren Baffin Island, north of the Labrador coast. They continued southeast along the coast to the big island of Newfoundland. At the northeastern tip of Newfoundland, they found a place to spend the winter. The Vikings called the place Vinland, which means "wine land."

The next summer Leif and his group went back to Greenland. He then let his brother, Thorvald, borrow his ship. Thorvald sailed west and found Leif's Vinland camp. Thorvald spent the summer exploring the coast, then spent the winter living in a hut Leif had built. The next summer he was killed in a battle with natives.

Thorvald's widow, Gudrid, went back to Greenland, but then she returned with her new husband to set up a permanent colony at Vinland. Later another group was led by Leif's sister, Freydis. Both Gudrid and Freydis were said to be hearty pioneers. Freydis not only fought natives, she also killed Viking enemies she had made.

Whether it was because of hostile natives, disease, or fights among the Vinland settlers, the colony did not last long. There is no recorded evidence of its existence past the year 1014.

There is also no evidence that the next Europe-

Leif Ericson, the famous Viking explorer.
It is believed that the Vikings were almost
certainly the first Europeans to establish
a settlement in America.

ans known to sail to the Americas nearly 500 years later knew anything about Vinland. It is true that the Vikings were almost certainly the first Europeans to create a settlement in America. But they were not really explorers—they were looking neither for new lands nor new routes to other lands. Their accomplishment did not change the way Europeans looked at the world. The conscious attempt by Europeans to figure out the shape of the part of the world that was unknown would not begin until the fifteenth century.

THE START OF THE AGE OF DISCOVERY

What is called Europe's Age of Discovery began on the southern tip of Portugal. In 1415 a young prince named Henry (1394–1460) decided to explore the west coast of Africa. He set up a center for explorers. It was located on high ground looking out on the Atlantic at the southeastern edge of Europe at a place called Sagres. Here Prince Henry set in motion the events that would change the way Europeans saw the world.

Henry himself did not travel on the ships sent out from Sagres. He was a member of a Roman Catholic religious order and lived a strict and simple life. To his center at Sagres he brought seafaring experts from all over the Mediterranean. Among them were ship builders, navigational instrument makers, astronomers, map makers, and ship's captains and navigators.

At the time Henry's expeditions got under way, Europe did not have much contact with far-off

Henry the Navigator

lands. Europeans knew parts of North Africa that bordered on the southern end of the Mediterranean. They knew parts of the Middle East situated on or very near the eastern end of the Mediterranean. But few people ever went beyond the Mediterranean.

Knowledge of the world began to increase as Henry—who would become known as Henry the Navigator—started sending out his ships. In the Atlantic he found and colonized the islands of Madeira and the Azores. But the most significant discoveries that resulted from his work came from his efforts in exploring ever farther to the south.

When Henry began his work at Sagres, no one from Europe was going very far south along the west coast of Africa. It was widely considered that the farthest south a ship could go was to just above Cape Bojador, which is located at the edge of the Sahara Desert of North Africa. This belief resulted from superstition. European sailors believed what North Africans told them about how no ship could ever survive a trip past Cape Bojador.

For years Henry sent dozens of ships south, and they all returned after turning back at the cape. Then in 1434 one of his captains, Gil Eanes, rounded the cape by avoiding the coastal currents; he took his ship west into the unknown ocean, and

People believed sea monsters inhabited the ocean and strange animals roamed the land. They also thought that south of the cape they would encounter a sun so hot it turned men black.

then headed south. He found that the stories he had heard about the southern waters were not true.

Now, year after year, Henry's ships were going farther and farther south. They went past the Sahara to points along the lush tropical coast below the desert. Soon the ships were returning with ivory, gold, and slaves.

Up until Henry's time, European shipbuilders had concentrated on ships to ply the Mediterranean. These ships were called "square-riggers" because they had square sails, suitable for sailing when the wind was going in the same direction the ship was going. But square sails are not so good when you have to follow a zigzag course against the wind.

At the shipyards operated by Henry the Navigator, smaller and more maneuverable ships were being built. The new ships were able to sail much more closely into the wind, and thus could be sent to places where it was not certain whether the wind would come from behind. Henry's new ships were rigged with triangular sails that made it easier to sail into the wind.

By the year 1460, when Henry died at the age of sixty-six, his ships had reached a point on the African coast more than 1,300 miles below Cape Bojador. His men controlled a busy trade along the African coast and had thus proved that exploration could result in making money.

There is no indication that Prince Henry had very precise ideas about what he expected to find before he began sending out his explorers. His men found and colonized the islands of Madeira and the Azores in the Atlantic. They set up trading posts in Africa. But these events did not end exploration.

Interest in finding a new route to the Far East increased after 1487. In that year the Portuguese explorer, Bartholomew Diaz, finally rounded the southern tip of Africa and found himself on the continent's east coast. His men, frightened by the unknown, insisted he return to Portugal without going farther. But now he had proven there was a way around Africa. He had proven it was possible to sail much farther east than anyone had known before.

At that time, European trade with the Far East—India, China, and the islands of what is now Indonesia—was controlled by merchants sailing for the powerful Italian city-state of Venice. They traded with ports in the eastern Mediterranean. The goods they sought, particularly silks and spices, had to come great distances overland by camel caravan.

Now the Portuguese and other Europeans were ready to enjoy the profits that could be made if a way were found to trade directly with the Far East. Diaz had pointed the way to a new route going east. Now there was also speculation that the Far East could be reached directly by heading not east, but west.

3 COLUMBUS: A NEW DIRECTION

Christopher Columbus, a map maker and mariner who was born in 1451 in the Italian city-state of Genoa, had several theories about the physical makeup of the world. Whether his theories were right or not, he was the man responsible for first bringing knowledge of America to Europe.

Like virtually all educated men of his time, he believed the world was round, and that thus you would eventually get to the Far East whether you sailed east or west. Here he was right. Where he was wrong was that he underestimated the earth's size. Japan, the first major country in the Far East to the west of Europe, is 10,000 miles from the Iberian Peninsula, which is shared by Portugal and Spain. Columbus estimated the distance at more like 3,000 miles. Also, he did not know that another continental land mass—North and South America—lay along the western route to Asia.

*Christopher Columbus is perhaps
the best known early explorer.*

Columbus settled in Portugal, where he tried to convince King John II to finance a westward trip to what he called "the Indies." When he was turned down in Portugal, he tried the kings of England and France. Then in 1492 he went to Spain, Portugal's great rival, to try his plan on the young monarchs King Ferdinand and Queen Isabella. They could not make up their minds. Frustrated, Columbus was about to board a ship to take his plan to the French again when he received a message saying Queen Isabella had decided she was in favor of his enterprise.

With three ships, the large *Santa María* and the caravel-type vessels *Niña* and *Pinta*, and about ninety men, Columbus sailed from the Spanish port of Palos on August 3, 1492, first to the Canary Islands, Spain's colony off the coast of North Africa. On September 6, 1492, he started west from the Canaries.

Navigation at this point was far from precise. The biggest advantage Columbus had over the Vikings of Leif Ericson's time was that he used a magnetic compass, which gave him a fairly clear idea of direction. Columbus also had some crude instruments that would measure the angle between the horizon and the sun or the horizon and the North Star. By taking that information and referring to a table, he could get an idea of his latitude—where he was north or south of the equator. But the readings often were not very accurate, and there were no instruments yet for measuring longitude—finding the point he had reached on the globe heading east to west.

Without more advanced aids to navigation, and relying on the wind for power, it took great skill for Columbus to follow a steady course across the Atlantic. He also needed great luck. As it turned out, he had found the best route for following the winds known as trade winds that blow steadily from the east across the ocean.

Columbus was lucky enough to have fair weather all the way. As the voyage wore on, however, his men got restless. By the time Columbus saw land on October 12, there were mutterings about turning back.

The land Columbus saw first was an island in the Bahamas, southeast of Florida, that he called San Salvador. He found Arawak tribesmen whom he called Indians, thinking he had reached "the Indies" in the Far East. (This is why native Americans are called Indians today, and the islands of the Caribbean the West Indies.)

As he moved on to larger islands, Columbus took Arawaks with him to serve as guides. From

*The landing of Columbus at
San Salvador in the Bahamas*

[23]

the Bahamas he sailed to Cuba and to Hispaniola, which today is divided between Haiti and the Dominican Republic.

He found more Indians on Cuba and Hispaniola, where he left behind a small colony of men anxious to get their hands on gold such as they had seen Indians wearing. Here at the outset, the Spanish began to enslave the Indians, treating them brutally and sending them to work in mines. Eventually, there were no Arawaks left.

Columbus remained convinced that he was in the Orient. When he sent out parties to look at native villages, he thought they would encounter representatives from important kingdoms of the Far East. One of the men he sent along spoke Arabic; he thought there would be people among the Chinese who knew Arabic from dealing with Arab traders. The parties he sent out bore letters directed to the emperor of China.

All they found were small villages of thatched huts. But Columbus remained convinced he had arrived at the eastern edge of Asia. He thought Cuba was part of the mainland. He had no idea that he was very close to two entire continents, North and South America, that were not part of Asia and did not appear on the world maps of the time.

After cruising through the lush green islands of the Bahamas and the northern Caribbean, Columbus returned to Europe early in 1493. Going back, he followed a route to the north of the route he had used coming across. He went first to the Azores, Portugal's islands out in the Atlantic that had been found by Henry the Navigator. He arrived in the Azores on February 18, 1493. He then went to Portugal, and a month later made his triumphal return to Spain. Just as he had found the best route west, following winds blowing out of the east, so had he found the best route east, following winds that blew from the west. Hundreds of years later, captains of sailing ships would still use the sea-lanes Columbus discovered.

Over the next twelve years, Columbus made three more trips across the Atlantic. These voyages were made less for exploration than to confirm that he had found the westward route to the Orient. On his second voyage, starting late in 1493, he arrived at the small Caribbean island of Dominica. He had seventeen ships this time and 1,200 men. He discovered his colony on Hispaniola had been wiped out by Indians and set up another. He did not return to Spain until 1496. On his third voyage, two years later, Columbus got down to Trinidad at the southern end of the Caribbean. He passed within sight of the South American mainland, but thought it was another island. On his final voyage, 1502–1504, he reached Central America.

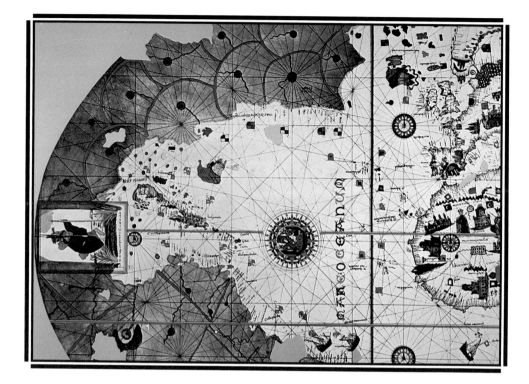

The upper part of the western half of the world.
Map drawn by Juan de la Cosa, navigator of
the Niña *on Columbus' second voyage of 1493.*

On that last voyage, Columbus concluded that
the land he found had not been known to map
makers in the past. He called it an "Other World."
But he decided that South America was a continua-
tion of the Malay Peninsula. Columbus was trying to

find a strait leading through the peninsula and surrounding islands that would get him to China and India.

When the explorer died in 1506, people in Spain were paying him little attention. He had not, as he had promised, opened up trade with the Far East. He had not brought back great treasure. His settlers had not gotten much gold out of Hispaniola. Columbus did not know that later he would be the man credited with finding what became known as the New World.

A businessman and navigator from the Italian state of Florence got the credit for figuring out that the new discoveries were not a part of Asia. It was for this man, Amerigo Vespucci (1454–1512), that America was named. He claimed to have gone along on four voyages to South America for the Spanish between about 1497 and 1502. Then, in 1504 and 1505, letters he was supposed to have written about his journeys were published in Florence. One of these letters says, "These regions we may rightly call . . . a New World, because our ancestors had no knowledge of them. . . . I have found a continent more densely peopled and abounding in animals than our Europe or Asia or Africa." Soon maps identified the new land mass as America.

Vespucci sailing to America

By now the Portuguese had succeeded in reaching India by going east, sailing around Africa. This was accomplished in 1498 by the explorer Vasco da Gama (ca. 1460–1524). Then in 1513, the Spaniard Vasco Núñez de Balboa walked across America's narrowest point at Panama and saw the Pacific Ocean. Balboa thought he was seeing a part of the

Balboa claiming the South Sea for Spain

Indian Ocean, but, in any case, his discovery demonstrated that Columbus was wrong in thinking the continent was part of the Indies.

The true significance of what Columbus had discovered became clearer after Ferdinand Magellan, a Portuguese sailing for Spain, set out with five ships in 1519 to look at the ocean Balboa had seen. The expedition accomplished the first circumnavigation of the earth.

The Portuguese now were colonizing Brazil, and the Spanish were bringing great wealth out of Mexico and were about to do the same with Peru. The attention of the seagoing world was focused on the Spanish treasure ships with their cargoes of gold and pearls.

But not everyone was looking south. Although in the north there were no great Indian empires or vast treasuries to be looted as in Mexico and Peru, no one knew this yet. The first great explorer captain to follow Columbus across the Atlantic chose a northern route.

4 JOHN CABOT'S NORTHERN VOYAGES

Not much is known about John Cabot (1450–1498), even though he is the man who established England's claims to North America. He had a son, Sebastian, who became an explorer too. It may be because Sebastian later tried to take credit for what his father accomplished that so few facts about John Cabot survive.

Cabot's father took him to Venice probably before he was ten years old. He became a citizen of Venice and a mariner, voyaging to the lands of the eastern Mediterranean, where the Venetians traded for Far Eastern goods brought overland by camel.

Like Columbus, Cabot developed his own theories about the world. He decided—incorrectly, as it turned out—that the great camel caravans carrying silk and spices came from the northeast edge of Asia, from what is now called Siberia. He began to think about getting to Asia following a northern route so as to get at the source of the goods. He tried without success to interest both Spain and Portugal in such a voyage.

The price of goods from Asia was particularly high in England because England was so far away from the eastern Mediterranean. Cabot reasoned that this would make England's King Henry VII particularly interested in his plan. Actually Columbus had tried and failed to get King Henry to sponsor his first voyage. But Cabot realized that Henry would now be more interested because of the excitement created by Columbus's success.

Cabot went to Bristol, an active port in the western part of England. It is believed that the wealthy merchants of Bristol, the men who controlled its shipping and trade, may have already sent at least one expedition to Newfoundland. They agreed to finance a trip across the Atlantic by Cabot. This made it easier for King Henry to sponsor the trip, which he did, because it would cost him nothing.

There are no surviving diaries or ship's logs written by either Cabot or the men who served with him. Still, historians have been able to put together an account of this first of the great northern voyages of the Age of Discovery.

Cabot sailed with a single ship called the *Matthew*. It was a small ship, probably similar to the

Niña, the ship Columbus sailed. It carried only eighteen men.

The *Matthew* left Bristol in late May 1497. It headed north up the coast of Ireland and then turned west. Because of headwinds, Cabot had to tack back and forth. Nevertheless, it was a rapid crossing, about the same as Columbus's, though because of the headwinds, only about half the distance was covered.

No one knows precisely where Cabot first saw land. Historians say it was somewhere between the Cape of Labrador to the north and Maine to the south. Some people, in reconstructing the crossing, believe Cabot made land almost precisely where Leif Ericson had landed five centuries earlier. This would be at the top of Newfoundland.

Men who talked with Cabot afterward report he promptly went ashore to lay claim to the land for England. This was apparently the only time he stepped on land. He did not see any natives, but he found evidence they were nearby. He found nets for catching fish, and snares set to catch game.

Cabot found none of the treasure that all the explorers sought. But he found one resource that would cause many men to make the crossing after him—codfish in great abundance. They were so

*Cabot and his men spent many weeks
exploring the coast on his journey.*

plentiful that they could be caught in places simply by lowering a basket over the *Matthew*'s side.

Cabot spent some weeks exploring the coast. On about July 20, he headed back to England. With the winds behind him now, he made the return crossing in about fifteen days, compared to about thirty-three days coming over.

Like Columbus before him, Cabot now boasted not that he had found an entirely new land but rather that he had found a new route to Asia.

He was received by King Henry, who rewarded him with money and approved another voyage. The king also approved Cabot's plan to set up a colony for the purpose of trading in Far Eastern spices.

In early May 1498, Cabot left Bristol to cross the Atlantic again. This time he had five ships. They carried food to last for a year and were well stocked with cloth and trinkets for trading with the natives. Traveling with Cabot were people to live in the colony he planned.

No one knows exactly what happened to Cabot. Soon after his departure from Bristol, one of the ships returned to Ireland. All the others, including the one Cabot was on, disappeared, never to be seen again.

In the quarter century after Cabot vanished, the emphasis on transatlantic exploration was centered on the great wealth that was being found in South America. But two ports continued to send out ships to North America. One was Terceira in the Azores, the Portuguese islands west of Portugal in the Atlantic. The other was Bristol, Cabot's jumping-off place.

Shortly after Columbus's first voyage, Pope Alexander VI, the leader of the Roman Catholic church, divided the unexplored world between Spain and Portugal. An imaginary line was drawn north to south. The Portuguese were given the right to any land east of that line; the Spanish, to land west of it. Other nations did not agree to this division, but for the moment Portugal, with its trade to the east, and Spain, looking west, were the two most important sea powers of Europe.

The eastern part of Brazil on South America's east coast jutted out over the line. Hence, Brazil was said to belong to Portugal, and before long the Portuguese were colonizing it. The rest of the new southern lands, including the islands of the Caribbean (the West Indies) and the rest of mainland South America, were west of the line and fell to the Spanish.

Soon the Portuguese began to wonder if the land of the codfish to the north was east of the line and therefore in their territory. Actually all of North

America was west of the line, but the Portuguese did not know this yet.

Not much is known about the voyages to North America that the Portuguese began making. They were conducted in great secrecy.

Reports from Portugal indicated that one of the explorers setting out from the Azores, Gaspar Corte Real, apparently reached Newfoundland in 1500. His trip was authorized by Portugal's King Manuel I, who apparently believed Cabot's codfish land was within the area the Pope had designated Portuguese territory.

The next year Corte Real made the crossing with three ships. The ship he was on was last seen heading south along the North American coast. The other two ships returned, carrying fifty-seven Indians who had been captured and made slaves, and, it was said, Venetian objects that had to have been left by Cabot.

Meanwhile at Bristol, three seafarers from the Azores joined to form a company with two Bristol merchants in 1501. The purpose of the company was exploration. King Henry VII authorized this group to conduct voyages of discovery in return for a ten-year monopoly the group would have on trade with any lands they found.

Like the expeditions from the Azores, little is

known about the trips they made. Among the gifts they brought back to the king were wildcats and three Indians, believed to have been from New-foundland.

Sebastian Cabot claimed to have traveled to Newfoundland looking for a strait that would lead through this land and on to China. It is not certain whether or not Sebastian Cabot actually went back to Newfoundland. But there was great interest in finding a strait to the east.

Now men who had no apparent interest in ex-ploration were heading for Newfoundland. They were fishermen going after the abundant codfish found in the area of the Grand Bank, a huge shoal to the southeast of Newfoundland. They went ashore to dry the fish they caught. Although they made no permanent settlements, the fishermen did begin trading for furs with the Indians.

First fishermen from Portugal and France began crossing to the Grand Bank. Later they were joined by fishermen from Bristol. They were there when the next round of exploration, this time by the French, began. By the seventeenth century, when settlement of North America by the Pilgrims and others began, there were many European seamen who had experienced the Atlantic crossing.

5 THE EARLY FRENCH EXPLORERS

In 1523 France had twice the population of Spain and Portugal combined, and six times the population of England. The country's ambitious leader, King Francis I, did not see why France should be overshadowed by Spain.

It was Spain that was getting rich from transatlantic exploration. In 1521 the Spanish conqueror Hernando Cortés had taken over the great Indian empire in Mexico. In 1522 the surviving ship of Magellan's round-the-world expedition had returned to Seville; heading out to the Far East, it had used a strait he found far south in South America that permitted him to sail from the Atlantic to the Pacific.

But King Francis wondered now if there were not a passage to Asia through America that was closer than the Strait of Magellan. Cabot and others from England and Portugal had done some searching far to the north. In the south the Spanish had searched all along the South American and Central American coasts and up along the coast of Florida. But there was no record yet of any explorer looking for a passage to the Pacific in the coastal area between what is now Georgia and what is now Maine.

A group of Italian bankers who lived in the French city of Lyons were also thinking about new routes to Asia. The sale of silk from China was a major business in Lyons. The bankers realized they could get silk much cheaper if they could bring it by ship directly from China rather than buying it from Venetians who got it in the Middle East. They turned to a skilled Italian ship's captain from Florence, Giovanni da Verrazano (ca. 1485–1528), who worked now for France. When he sailed, Verrazano was backed both by the merchants and the French king.

Because he was commissioned by the king, Verrazano had the use of a 100-ton ship, the *Dolphin*, which was loaned to him by the French navy. In late 1523 he set out in the *Dolphin* to follow a route somewhat north of the route Columbus had used on his first voyage just over thirty years earlier. The *Dolphin* left the Portuguese island of Madeira on January 17, 1524. At first Verrazano enjoyed the easterly trade winds that had aided Columbus. On

Verrazano, a skillful captain, had many encounters with Indians on his voyages.

February 24 he hit a storm and changed his course to head farther north.

On March 1 he reached land at what is now called Cape Fear in the southern part of North Carolina. Here he met with Indians, who shared their food with him and his men. He decided they were racially similar in appearance to the people he would expect to find on the edge of China. He sailed south, then turned north again for fear he would come into conflict with the Spanish. Farther up the coast, he traded small manufactured goods with Indians. When one of his men was hit violently by a wave while returning to the ship, the Indians rescued him.

At North Carolina's Cape Hatteras, Verrazano looked at the banks surrounding Pamlico Sound and decided that what he was seeing was a narrow strip of land between the Atlantic and Pacific oceans. For a hundred years, mapmakers, following his account, would show Pamlico Sound as part of the Pacific.

Verrazano became the first European to sail into New York Bay. He anchored there, probably off Staten Island or Brooklyn. Today a great bridge, named after Verrazano, links these two places.

While anchored in Narragansett Bay at Rhode Island, as at New York Bay, Verrazano received

Indians who came out in dugout canoes. An Indian piloted the *Dolphin* through Narragansett Bay. (This was the same tribe of Indians, the Wampanoag, that would befriend the Pilgrims in the following century.)

It was now early May. The *Dolphin* continued along the coast, past Cape Cod and the islands of Nantucket and Martha's Vineyard in Massachusetts. The ship crossed Massachusetts Bay and hit the coast of Maine.

Verrazano explored the length of the Maine coast, continued up to Newfoundland, and then headed east. In just over two weeks, the *Dolphin* arrived, on July 8, 1524, back at the French port of Dieppe.

Verrazano made some major miscalculations in trying to figure out what he had found. He thought the distance to the Far East was much less than it actually was, and he thought he had covered a greater distance sailing west than he had. He made the mistake of concluding that North Carolina narrowed down to a strip of land between the Atlantic and Pacific oceans. But he did insist that what he had found was a New World, not just a part of Asia.

His return to the New World was delayed because France was fighting a war in Europe. But in

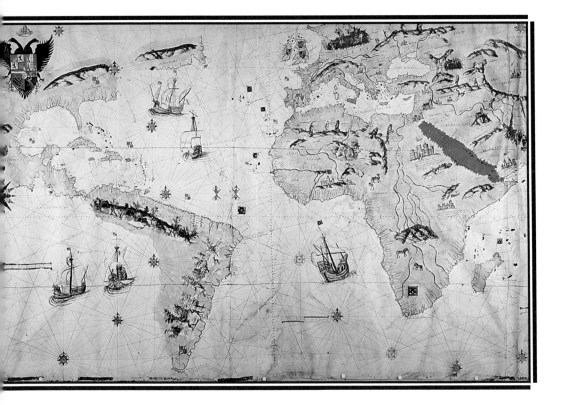

*This is how the world looked in
the 1520s. World map of Juan Vespucci.*

the spring of 1527, Verrazano sailed again, this time reaching Brazil, where he opened up trade for France. The next year he sailed to Florida, and then was killed in the Caribbean in an attack by fierce Carib Indians.

King Francis continued to dream of much more than trade with someone else's American possession. He still hoped France would find a passage to the Far East. And he began to dream of a French empire in North America.

The dream now was that such an empire could be established in the far north. The man charged with this mission was Jacques Cartier (1491–1557), a master mariner from a family of mariners at the port of St. Malo. In the three voyages he made to places in what became Canada, Cartier established France's claims to territory in the New World.

From the start, Cartier had the backing of King Francis. On his first voyage, he left St. Malo April 20, 1534, with two ships, each about the same size as Verrazano's *Dolphin*. Twenty days later, they reached Cape Bonavista in Newfoundland. Cartier explored the south coast of Labrador, the west coast of Newfoundland, and the area of the Gaspé Peninsula at the mouth of the St. Lawrence River.

He made contact with a large party of Huron Indians. Their chief, Donnaconna, let Cartier carry off his two teenage sons, Domagaya and Taignoaguy. With the Indian boys, who were dressed in European clothes now, Cartier got back to St. Malo in three weeks, arriving on September 5, 1534. Almost immediately, he was planning his return.

Cartier's landing in 1534

The Indian chief and his sons had been telling tall tales about a mythical kingdom called Saguenay, a place of fabulous wealth, in the interior of Canada. Cartier's goal was to discover Saguenay and take it over for France the way Spain had taken over rich empires in Mexico and Peru.

For his second trip, Cartier had the use of three French naval ships. He left Dieppe on May 19, 1535. This time Cartier was charged with exploring to the west of Newfoundland.

Because of bad weather, the crossing took fifty days. Cartier rounded Newfoundland to the north. He proceeded to the mouth of the St. Lawrence, which he named on August 10, the feast of St. Lawrence. He started up the river to look for Saguenay. He also sailed up a smaller river, which he called the Saguenay. He went up the St. Lawrence to the site of the future city of Montreal. He headed back to the site of Quebec City, where he spent the winter.

Cartier had brought Domagaya and Taignoaguy, the two Indian boys, along as guides, but he still had not found Saguenay. There was no such place. However, he still believed it existed. In the spring, he was ready to go back to France to organize a bigger expedition. He decided to take along a more important Indian this time to tell about the kingdom. He kidnapped the father of his two teenage guides. On June 19, 1536, Cartier set sail, and was in St. Malo on July 15. With him he had the chief, Donnaconna, and nine other Indians.

During the five years between Cartier's second and third trips, plans were laid to set up a colony in North America. King Francis was now convinced that a New World Empire would make him more powerful than the Spanish, who were getting rich looting Mexico and Peru, and the Portuguese, who had a thriving trade in slaves with Africa and in spices with islands that are today part of Indonesia.

Donnaconna was taken before the king to repeat his stories about the kingdom of Saguenay. He told the king what Francis wanted to hear. In addition to its supposed mineral wealth, Donnaconna told Francis, Saguenay also had fruits such as were found in places far to the south, and the sort of spices found in the Far East.

The king sent back a joint expedition that started out in 1541. Cartier and a nobleman, Sieur de Roberval, were to take ten ships. However, Roberval was delayed, so Cartier set out with five ships. Roberval later joined him. Since the idea was to set up a colony, there were some women on board the ships.

A map of the world by Battista Agnese that traces the Spanish treasure fleet's route around the world, in about 1545

Again they searched the St. Lawrence for the kingdom, and, of course, failed to find it. Cartier returned to France the following year, Roberval with the last of the would-be colonists in 1543.

France now abandoned its attempts to colonize Canada until the next century. But its claims to the territory had been made.

6

ENGLAND AND THE NORTHWEST PASSAGE

In the second half of the sixteenth century, the great voyages of transatlantic exploration were conducted by the English. For a time after the Cabots, England had neglected the Americas. But during the reign of Queen Elizabeth I (which is called the Elizabethan period), from 1558 to 1603, the English were suddenly moving out into the world as they had never done before. For the first time they began to challenge the power of Spain at sea.

There were many battles at sea as England and other powers tried to grab some of Spain's New World treasure. But the English were particularly active in the north, far away from the areas of Spain's power. Not interested yet in establishing American colonies, they were still searching for a sea route through the Americas to the Far East. Like other monarchs before her, Queen Elizabeth thought the discovery of a direct route to the Far

East would push her country ahead of Spain. In other words, the English were still searching for the Northwest Passage.

One who took up the quest was Sir Humfry Gilbert, a soldier and a writer as well as a mariner. In 1566, he wrote a paper attempting to prove there was a Northwest Passage to China. It had a great influence on the mariners of the day.

Then Martin Frobisher, a blunt professional sailor, explored the coast of Labrador searching for the passage. In 1577 he took a rock that he thought contained gold back to London. It was worthless; he had discovered neither wealth nor the passage. But the search went on.

In 1583 Gilbert sailed with his small flagship, the *Squirrel*, and four other ships, hoping to start a colony. He arrived in Newfoundland and formally took possession of it for England. He told the fishermen he encountered there that henceforth they would have to obey Queen Elizabeth. He was on his way home in rough seas when sailors on one of his ships saw the *Squirrel* vanish from sight. Plans for a colony were abandoned.

Meanwhile, in 1579 England's Sir Francis Drake had searched for a passage from the other side of the continent. Drake, who had sailed through the

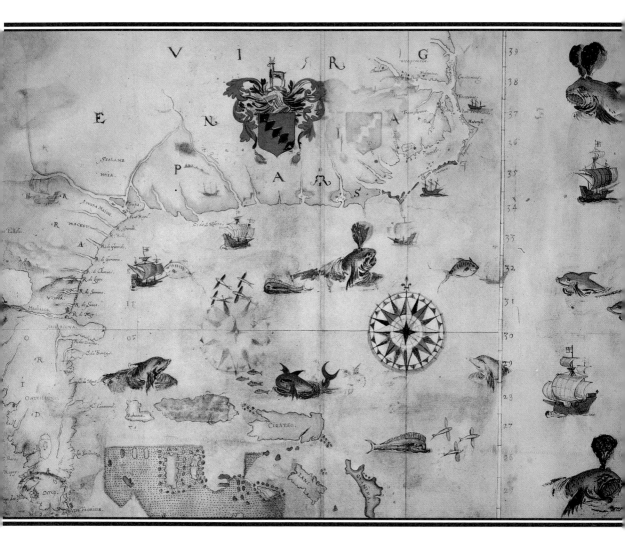

*A map of North America from Florida to the
Chesapeake Bay, around 1585, by John White*

The voyage of Henry Hudson and the Half
Moon *along the Hudson River in 1609*

Strait of Magellan at the tip of South America, went all the way up the coast to anchor, apparently, at what is now called San Francisco Bay. He claimed the area for England, though it was the Spanish from Mexico who would come first to colonize it.

Although no entrance to any strait was found on either end of the continent, the search was not abandoned yet. It continued on past Queen Elizabeth's time. Henry Hudson—who in 1609 had sailed for the Dutch up the river that bears his name—sailed for the English in 1610, looking for the Northwest Passage. He found the great bay in eastern Canada that was named for him.

In a sense, the search continued until early in the twentieth century when the Norwegian explorer Roald Amundsen cut through ice in the Arctic, taking a fishing ship from the Atlantic to the Pacific. But this was not a practical route for ocean commerce.

There was no Northwest Passage. But in the course of searching for it, much of the east coast of America had been mapped.

7

THE EXPLORERS' ACCOMPLISHMENTS

Not one of the European explorers who crossed the Atlantic to North America in the Age of Discovery found precisely what he was seeking. None found a strait permitting ships to pass through the continent to China. None found an empire full of treasure waiting to be looted. And none established settlements.

Moreover, none of the great explorers left a permanent colony in what would become Canada and the United States.

What settlement did come in the rest of the sixteenth century had little significance for the continent's future. The only settlement that lasted was the town of St. Augustine in Florida, founded in 1565 by the Spanish.

In the 1560s the French tried to plant a trading post colony on the Florida coast, but the colonists were attacked and killed by the Spanish. In the 1580s England's Sir Walter Raleigh, a half brother of the explorer Sir Humfrey Gilbert, sent out settlers

Sir Walter Raleigh with his son. Raleigh started the colony of Roanoke in Virginia.

A new description of America,
from Abraham Ortelius' Theatrum
Orbis Terrarum, *1570*

to start the colony of Roanoke on an island off North Carolina. When an English ship returned there after three years, all of the colonists had vanished, presumed to have starved or been killed or kidnapped by Indians.

But in the next century, the English established coastal settlements that would last. First there were colonial outposts in Massachusetts and Virginia, and then settlements all the way from Maine to Georgia. In the far south, Florida remained Spanish for the time. But in the far north, in eastern Canada, the French now started coastal settlements and left outposts all through the Great Lakes region.

The English claimed a right to settle because of Cabot, the French because of Cartier. For a time the Dutch, basing claims on Henry Hudson's first voyage, had New York.

The explorers themselves may not have found what they wanted. But they had gone off into the unknown and spread tales at home of new lands. They thus set off events that would transform the wilderness continent that had been found by mistake as Europeans looked for a route to China.

FOR FURTHER READING

Boorstin, Daniel J. *The Discoverers.* New York: Random House, 1983.

Elliott, John Huxtable. *The Old World and the New 1492–1650.* Cambridge, Mass.: Cambridge University Press, 1970.

Maddocks, Melvin. *The Atlantic Crossing.* New York: Time-Life Books, 1981.

Morison, Samuel Eliot. *The European Discovery of America: The Northern Voyages.* New York: Oxford University Press, 1971.

———. *The European Discovery of America: The Southern Voyages.* New York: Oxford University Press, 1974.

Sanger, P. H. *The Age of the Vikings.* New York: St. Martin's Press, 1972.

INDEX